D1109725

THE ARTFUL ASTROLOGER

VIRGO

Lee Holloway

Gramercy Books
New York • Avenel

To my children

A Friedman Group Book

Copyright ©1993 by Michael Friedman Publishing Group
All rights reserved.

This 1993 edition is published by Gramercy Books,
distributed by Outlet Book Company, Inc.,
a Random House Company, 40 Engelhard Avenue,
Avenel, New Jersey 07001.

Printed and bound in Singapore

Library of Congress Cataloging–in–Publication Data

Holloway, Lee.
    The artful astrologer. Virgo / by Lee Holloway.
        p.   cm.
    ISBN 0-517-08254-3
    1. Virgo (Astrology)   I. Title.
  BF1727.4H65   1993
  133.5'2—dc20
                              93-24865
                              CIP

8 7 6 5 4 3 2 1

CONTENTS

6 Introduction

14 The Planets

16 The Zodiac Signs

20 Your Sun Sign Profile

28 Compatibility With the Other Signs

44 Birthdays of Famous Virgos

48 About the Author

Photo Credits

Symbolic rendering of a seventeenth-century astrologer.

INTRODUCTION

I s astrology bunk, or is there something to it? If astrology is utter nonsense, why have so many of the world's finest thinkers, including Johannes Kepler, Copernicus, Isaac Newton, Carl Jung, and Goethe, turned to astrology for information and guidance over the centuries?

Some people may scoff when astrology is mentioned, but even these skeptics are usually inquisitive about their signs. Whenever I attend a dinner party, I ask the host not to mention that I am an astrologer—at least not until dessert— because the conversation invariably turns to astrolo-

In the middle ages, the wealthy consulted astrologers regularly.

gy. When people learn that I am an astrologer, they first try to get me to tell them about their signs and what lies in store for them. Then, in a subtle way, they bring up the next bit of business, which usually concerns a loved one. Finally, as you've probably guessed, they want to know whether the two signs get along.

We humans are an inquisitive lot—we are eager to learn more about our friends, family, lovers, and employers. Astrology is one way to satisfy that natural curiosity.

In the not too distant past, only royalty, heads of state, and the very rich consulted with astrologers; such consultation was a privilege of the elite. Today, astrology is a source of information and fascination for millions; astrological columns can be found in major newspapers and magazines all over the world.

Astrology is not a form of magic. It is a science. Put simply, it is a practical application of astronomy that links the stars and planets with our daily lives. A horoscope is a picture of the stars and planets at a given time, such as that of a person's birth. By examining each planet's position and the relationships of all of the planets to each other at a specific moment, an astrologer can determine your basic personality or predict a general course of events. Perhaps the noted Swiss psychologist Carl Jung summed up the concept of astrology best when he said, "Whatever is born or done at this moment, has the qualities of this moment in time." Astrologers form a continuous link with the past, and each human being, although unique, is part of nature and the universe.

Unfortunately, some people have the misconception that astrology dictates who they are and how their life has to be.

This chart dates back to fourteenth-century Italy. The inside circles represent the element, ruling body part, and orientation of each respective sign.

Medieval illuminated manuscript of biblical characters observing the stars.

Nothing could be further from the truth. Astrology does not remove our free will; it simply points out our basic nature and how we are likely to react in certain circumstances. Astrology indicates strengths and weaknesses, talents and abilities, difficulties and opportunities. It is always up to the individual to use this information, and to live his or her life accordingly, or to disregard it.

Like other sciences, astrology's origins date back thousands of years. There is evidence that primitive peoples recorded the phases of the Moon by carving notches on reindeer bones, and that they may have linked the Moon's movement with the tides, or the snow's melting in spring with the rising of the constellation now known as Aries. As early as 2000 B.C., astrologers were using instruments—carved out of granite or fashioned from brass or copper—to observe and calculate the positions of constellations. These calculations were surprisingly accurate, even by today's standards.

Over time, astrological calculations were refined and the planets were named. The Babylonians were the first to describe the natural zodiac, and their first horoscope dates back to 409 B.C. Centuries ago, people began to examine the stars' potential impact on human emotions, spirit, and intellect. Today, astrology is so deeply embedded in our culture and language that we rarely give it a second thought. The

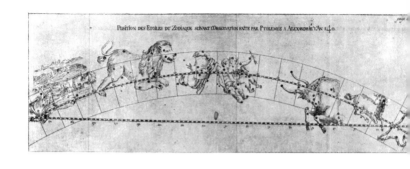

The twelve zodiacal constellations as drawn according to Ptolemy's descriptions.

days of the week , for example, have their roots in astrology. Sunday is derived from "Sun Day," Monday from "Moon Day," Tuesday from "Tiwe's Day," Wednesday from "Woden's Day," Thursday from "Thor's Day," Friday from "Frigga's Day," and Saturday from "Saturn's Day." Lunacy, which originally referred to so-called full-moon madness, now encompasses all varieties and forms of mental illness.

Before we begin, I'd like to touch upon one final point. Throughout this book, you'll see references to "rulers." A ruler, in astrological terms, has the same meaning as it does in human society; "ruler" refers to the planet that governs or co-governs an astrological sign (see pages 14–15) or to the constellation rising at the birth of a person or event. Everything has a moment of birth: people, places, profes-

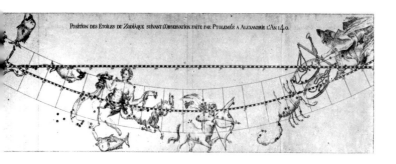

POSITION DES ETOILES DU ZODIAQUE SUIVANT L'OBSERVATION FAITE PAR PTOLEMÉE A ALEXANDRIE L'AN 140.

sions, even ideas; it would take volumes to show you what persons, places, and things your sign rules, but a small sampling has been included here. For example, different parts of the body have rulers, and that body part is often a point of strength and weakness. Gemstones and colors have also been assigned to each sign, although there are varying opinions about the validity of these less important areas. (It should also be noted here that the gemstone assigned to a particular sign does not correspond to the birthstone assigned to that month.) Generally, however, colors and gemstones are said to reflect the specific energy of each sign.

May *The Artful Astrologer* enlighten and entertain you.

Lee Holloway

THE PLANETS

The **SUN** symbolizes the life force that flows through everything. It rules the sign of Leo and represents ego, will, identity, and consciousness.

The **MOON** symbolizes emotions and personality. It rules the sign of Cancer and represents feeling, instinct, habit, childhood, mother, sensitivity, and receptivity.

MERCURY symbolizes the mind and communication. It rules the signs of Gemini and Virgo and represents thought, learning, communication, reason, speech, youth, and perception.

VENUS symbolizes love and attraction. It rules the signs of Taurus and Libra and represents harmony, values, pleasure, comfort, beauty, art, refinement, and balance.

MARS symbolizes action and drive. It rules the sign of Aries and represents energy, the sex drive, initiative, the ability to defend oneself, resilience, and conflict.

JUPITER symbolizes expansion and growth. It rules the sign of Sagittarius and represents higher thought and learning, principles, beliefs, optimism, abundance, idealism, and morals.

SATURN symbolizes universal law and reality. It rules the sign of Capricorn and represents structure, discipline, limitation, restriction, fear, authority figures, father, teachers, and time.

The nine planets that comprise our solar system: Mercury, Venus, Earth, Mars, Saturn, Jupiter, Uranus, Neptune, and Pluto.

URANUS symbolizes individuality and change. It rules the sign of Aquarius and represents intuition, genius, insight, reform, unconventionality, and freedom.

NEPTUNE symbolizes compassion and spirituality. It rules the sign of Pisces and represents the search for the divine, intuition, dreams, illusion, imagination, and confusion.

PLUTO symbolizes transformation and regeneration. It rules the sign of Scorpio and represents power, death and rebirth, the subconscious, elimination, obsession, and purging.

THE ZODIAC SIGNS

Just as there are twelve months in the year, there are twelve astrological signs in the zodiac. The word "zodiac" comes from the Greek *zoidiakos*, which means "circle of animals" and refers to a band of fixed stars that encircles the earth. The twelve signs are divided into four elements: fire, air, earth, and water. The three signs within an element share many similarities, but each sign in the zodiac is unique. The following section is a brief summary of the qualities of the signs born under each element. (The terms "positive" and "negative" as they are used here describe qualities, and are not judgments.)

The fire signs are Aries, Leo, and Sagittarius. They are termed positive and extroverted. They are warm, creative, outgoing, expressive, idealistic, inspirational, and enthusiastic.

The air signs are Gemini, Libra, and Aquarius. They are termed positive and extroverted. They are social, outgoing, objective, expressive, and intellectual.

The earth signs are Taurus, Virgo, and Capricorn. They are termed negative and introverted. They are practical, conservative, reserved, traditional, and deliberate.

The water signs are Cancer, Scorpio, and Pisces. They are termed negative and introverted. They are sensitive, emotional, imaginative, and intuitive.

The fire signs:

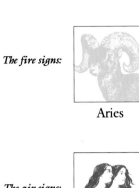

Aries   Leo   Sagittarius

The air signs:

Gemini   Libra   Aquarius

The earth signs:

Taurus   Virgo   Capricorn

The water signs:

Cancer   Scorpio   Pisces

V i r

♍

Symbol: Virgin

Planetary ruler: Mercury

Element: Earth

Rules in the body: Intestines

Day of the week: Wednesday

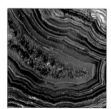

Gem: Agate

Color: Beige

Key Word: Analyze

YOUR SUN SIGN PROFILE

Are you the type of person who goes crazy when a picture hangs unevenly? Do you unconsciously pick the lint off fabric, be it clothing or a tablecloth? Do you meticulously attend to the smallest details? This is what a Virgo does best. It could be said that Virgo is the inspector of the zodiac, for no other sign rivals Virgo's extraordinary powers of observation, discrimination, and analysis; this sign's key words are "I analyze." Gifted with objectivity and precision, Virgo is an industrious worker who completes whatever task is at hand with efficiency and economy.

Virgos seek nothing less than perfection and always try to deliver their best. They may seem judgmental at times, but they are actually gentle souls who thrive on being of service to

ASTRONOMICAL FACT

Mercury, Virgo's ruler, is the fastest-moving planet in our solar system, whizzing around the Sun in just eighty-eight days, one-fourth the time it takes the Earth to do so. Mercury is the ruler of all communications.

others (Mother Theresa is a Virgo). But their problem, of course, is trying to attain perfection in an imperfect world; that's why they are often so critical of themselves and those around them. The ability to see perfection and the drive to attain it is at the core of all Virgos, which is why they tend to worry and struggle with bouts of insecurity.

Virgos often vacillate between doing far too much and not moving at all, and that inertia is usually due to mental exhaustion. Moderation doesn't seem to exist for this mentally restless sign. Ruled by Mercury, the planet governing thought and communication and the fastest-moving planet in the solar system, Virgos are so driven and mentally quick that it may seem as though they are tied to a rocket. They tend to be high-strung because they often feel that they have so much to do and so little time to do it in. And when they're really worried about getting everything done, they may seem like walking nerve ends! Even when Virgos appear calm, they are

VOCALLY GIFTED VIRGOS

Frankie Avalon, Brook Benton, Maurice Chevalier, Patsy Cline, Elvis Costello, Gloria Estefan, Michael Feinstein, José Feliciano, Buddy Holly, Chrissie Hynde, Michael Jackson, Joan Jett, B.B. King, Maria Muldaur, Yma Sumac, Mel Torme, Barry White, Hank Williams, Paul Williams

Freddie Mercury

Michael Jackson is industrious, a perfectionist, and shy—all key Virgo traits.

endlessly weighing and analyzing, seeking the best solution to some problem. When they're set upon a task, nothing else exists until they've done a bang-up job of completing it.

It follows, therefore, that when it comes to their careers, Virgos usually accomplish more by accident than other signs do by design. Virgos just can't help it; they simply have a natural sense for the best, fastest, and most resourceful way of doing a job. You go crazy if you don't have something to do, and you usually can and do handle more responsibility than your coworkers. You may bemoan the fact that you are overloaded and overworked, but inwardly you thrive on heavy responsibility. Actually, you function best under pressure. A Virgo is truly an employer's dream come true; no one works harder or longer, and a Virgo often worries about a job as if he or she owned the company.

Blessed with a fine intellect, excellent reasoning abilities, and high standards, Virgos are good administrators and excel at many professions, including accounting, editing, illustration, and literary or film criticism. Virgos also have a keen interest in health and diet, so medicine, nutrition, and owning a food-

Fay Wray

**VIRGOS OFTEN
HAVE A COOL,
REFINED BEAUTY**

Anne Archer
Lauren Bacall
Shari Belafonte-Harper
Ingrid Bergman
Jacqueline Bisset
Greta Garbo
Catherine Oxenberg
Raquel Welch

Sophia Loren

related business may be gratifying work. Because Virgos are basically shy, they would rather not be in the limelight or at the head of an organization, even though they might have the requisite talent and skills.

As for love and romance, this seemingly shy sign can be a bit of a flirt and has great sexual appeal. Sean Connery, Sophia Loren, and Ingrid Bergman are just a few examples of the passionate fire that burns beneath that often cool Virgo exterior. Never forget for a moment that Virgo is an earth sign first and last, and earth is one of the most sensual elements in the zodiac. Yes, Virgos may appear collected, but when they're in love they apply the same zeal to romance that they do to work and accomplishment. Virgos can be quite skillful lovers—after all, they seek perfection in whatever they do. Their humility and refinement restrains them from crowing about such private matters, but they can woo with the best of

A DAY IN THE LIFE OF A VIRGO?

It was about eleven o'clock in the morning, mid-October, with the sun not shining and a look of hard rain in the clearness of the foothills. I was wearing my powder-blue suit, with dark blue shirt, tie and display handkerchief, black brogues, black wool socks with dark blue clocks on them. I was neat, clean, shaved and sober, and I didn't care who knew it.

— Raymond Chandler,
The Big Sleep

Ingrid Bergman

Sean Connery

ACTORS WHO PROJECT THAT REFINED VIRGO AIR

Anne Archer
Lauren Bacall
Anne Bancroft
Jacqueline Bissett
Maurice Chevalier
Claudette Colbert
Greta Garbo
Jeremy Irons
Amy Irving
Anne Jackson
Hedy Lamarr
Sophia Loren
Catherine Oxenberg

Gene Kelly

VIRGOS WITH THAT PERFECTLY CRITICAL WIT

Sid Caesar
Jane Curtin
Anne Meara
Bill Murray
Peter Sellers

Lily Tomlin

them. Of course, they might require the ideal setting... everything neat, tidy, an freshly dusted!

Virgos make for devoted friends and lovers, although they have been known to criticize their loved ones, sometimes very heavily, in order to help them improve themselves. Those closest to them know that they intend not one bit of malice, for if they hurt anyone they care about, they feel devastated and will immediately apologize and do everything they can to make amends. Many things can be said about Virgo's judgmental nature, but, above all, Virgo is bright and kind-hearted, and wants only the best for those he or she loves. And it would be hard to find a better companion than a Virgo.

Like every sign, Virgo has positive and negative attributes, and the ability to choose which qualities to express. As a

Virgo, if you don't act according to your best qualities, others may see you as critical and cold, or as having a misplaced focus, tending to give priority to petty details rather than to important matters. You need only apply your considerable ability to analyze matters to discover the right course of action. It is essential for you to remember that the mind is a good servant but a terrible master, and that the happiness you seek comes from the heart, with a little help from the head along the way.

In her role as the genie in the hit television series I Dream of Jeannie, *Virgo Barbara Eden brought her sign's clever, flirtatious nature to the fore.*

COMPATIBILITY WITH THE OTHER SIGNS

In nature, some elements are more compatible and blend more easily than others, like fire and air, and earth and water; the same holds true in astrology. Therefore, some astrological signs naturally interact more harmoniously than others.

The information in this section describes how Virgo tends to relate to the other signs of the zodiac. It provides guidelines to the potential

> **FIRST WORD PROBABLY LEARNED BY A VIRGO**
>
> Why?

strengths and weaknesses of a relationship between two signs. But remember, these are only guidelines. In the final analysis, the choice is yours.

As an earth sign, Virgo is most compatible with the other earth signs, Taurus and Capricorn. The natural rapport shared by the earth signs is due to their many intellectual and emotional similarities.

The water signs Cancer and Scorpio are also very good partners for Virgo. Although Pisces is also a water sign, it is Virgo's polar opposite in the zodiac, so the relationship would be a bit more challenging than one with the other water signs. In nature, "water nourishes earth, while earth gives water form," and the same is true in astrology. This is the reason water and earth signs are basically compatible.

The air signs—Gemini, Libra, and Aquarius—make less suitable partners for Virgo. They thrive on changeability, and this lack of consistency tends to really frazzle Virgo, who thrives on order and practicality. The air signs are also sociable, while Virgo is shy and often uncomfortable with new people and at social gatherings.

The fire signs—Aries, Leo, and Sagittarius—are less likely partners for Virgo than the water and earth signs. Fire signs are assertive and enthusiastic, and have a great tendency to act and speak on impulse. Virgos are refined, prefer to act according to a plan, and, because of their great critical abilities, tend to see the bad before the good.

> **GIFTS SURE TO PLEASE VIRGOS**
>
> crossword puzzles, jigsaw puzzles, and brain twisters; organizers for home and office; pocket planners; calculators; how-to books on efficiency and psychology; relaxation tapes; cookbooks; health food; baskets of flowers; tickets to a self-improvement seminar; cassettes or CDs; anything beige

TAURUS AND VIRGO

Taurus (April 21–May 21) and Virgo are highly compatible because they both possess practical and conservative temperaments. Taurus' soothing and stable nature will help offset Virgo's nervousness. Taurus is slow and steady like the Tortoise, while Virgo is more like the Hare, always rushing to accomplish some task or goal.

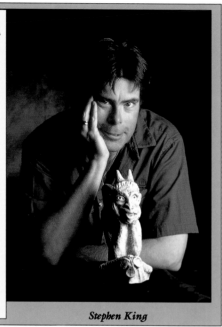

VIRGOS ARE WOOED BY ELOQUENCE. HERE ARE A FEW WHO CAN TURN A PHRASE

Cleveland Amory
Edgar Rice Burroughs
Agatha Christie
Roald Dahl
Fannie Flagg
William Golding
O. Henry
Oliver Wendell Holmes
Ken Kesey
William X. Kienzle
John Knowles
D. H. Lawrence
Kate Millett
William Saroyan
Mary Shelley
Upton Sinclair
Leo Tolstoy
H. G. Wells

Stephen King

Taurus' steadiness and easygoing attitude can help to steady Virgo, who is constantly worrying, and weighing and analyzing ideas. Virgo's quick mind and wit will fascinate Taurus, who tends to think and act with greater deliberation. Because there is a strong common ground and a nice balance between the two personalities, this relationship has fine long-term potential.

Twiggy

CAPRICORN AND VIRGO

Because they are both reserved, pragmatic, and need security, Capricorn (December 22– January 21) and Virgo are also extremely well-suited partners. Capricorn likes to be in the driver's seat, since this sign is most comfortable managing situations, while Virgo's natural inclination is to serve others; there won't be many power struggles in this pairing. Capricorn is a go-getter and Virgo is no slouch, so dedication to work will be understood and supported in this union as well. Virgo's analytical and organizational abilities can enhance Capricorn's plans for success. These two signs are well-matched in terms of intellect and drive.

VIRGO AND VIRGO

 Two Virgos can be a good match, for they have similar natures. After all, it's easy to understand someone who is so much like yourself. However, similarity can breed problems. Virgos can be the most caring, down-to-earth people imaginable, but their tendency to be highly critical of those they love can cause strife. Two Virgos will need to keep their ideas for improving one another to a minimum—Virgos are already hard enough on themselves! To avoid wearing each other out, they will also need to temper their tendency to worry too much.

SOME CITIES RULED BY VIRGO

Baghdad, Iraq
Basel, Switzerland
Boston, Massachusetts
Brindisi, Italy
Bury, England
Los Angeles, California
Paris, France

The Eiffel Tower in Paris, France.

Virgos are not too fond of socializing, and Greta Garbo certainly was one Virgo who wanted to be left alone.

CANCER AND VIRGO

Cancer (June 22–July 23) and Virgo are a good mix. Cancer is naturally nurturing and receptive, and can soothe Virgo's tense, insecure nature. Cancer is also extremely feeling-oriented, experiencing almost as many highs and lows as there are hours in the day. Virgo can help to balance this moodiness with typical objectivity and rational approach to matters. Because Cancer is so emotional, Virgo will have to curb the tendency to judge others. But the rewards for doing so will be worth the effort, for a Cancer can be very giving and loving when treated with sensitivity.

Jacqueline Bisset has the cool, refined looks Virgos are often noted for.

SCORPIO AND VIRGO

 Scorpio (October 23–November 21) is another good match for Virgo. Virgo is highly intellectual and goal-oriented; Scorpio is very emotional and has a strong drive to attain a position of power. Virgo needs a partner with drive to focus his or her vast efficiency, while Scorpio needs someone to handle tedious tasks with logic and organization. Virgo has no great desire to be in control—one of Scorpio's greatest needs—so power struggles are unlikely. Virgo's practical approach can help Scorpio make decisions, too. Scorpio tends to be jealous, but Virgo is faithful and trustworthy, so this would allay Scorpio's concerns. Virgo loves to talk, but Scorpio is very private, often finding it difficult to articulate feelings; communication would be a facet of the relationship that would require work. On the whole, these two can enhance each other's lives in interesting ways.

PISCES AND VIRGO

 Pisces (February 19–March 20) opposes Virgo in the zodiac, and astrological opposites often attract. However, there is always some tension with polar opposites, for they are very different souls. Pisces is a dreamer; Virgo is ruled by reason and logic. Pisces is fanciful and emotional; Virgo is rooted in reality and practicality. Pisces' world is a bit fuzzy and has blurred boundaries; Virgo's world is black and white, and has clear parameters. Although these two signs are radically different, each has something to offer the other. Pisces could help Virgo see the world less harshly and precisely, and Virgo could help Pisces see the world a little more realistically. They can inspire and be inspired by each other, but only if they accept their differences.

GEMINI AND VIRGO

Gemini (May 22–June 21) and Virgo share a ruling planet, Mercury, so Virgo has better potential with Gemini than with the other air signs. Both Virgo and Gemini have the gift of gab, and are quick-witted and restless, but that's where the similarity ends. Gemini loves to talk, but doesn't always mean what he or she says, while Virgo is sin-

**SOME COUNTRIES
RULED BY VIRGO**

Assyria
Babylonia
Brazil
Croatia
Mesopotamia
Rhodesia
Turkey
Uruguay

Rio de Janeiro, Brazil, at night.

cere and expects to be treated similarly by others. Virgo is faithful and straightforward, while Gemini can be flirtatious and fickle. Virgo may be irked by Gemini's capriciousness, viewing it as superficial and immature, while Gemini may be frustrated and bored by Virgo's deep need for order and consistency. Curiously, these two signs are often attracted to each other. Compromise and adjustment are critical for a happy relationship between these two intellects.

Virgos thrive on work, and Jimmy Connors has labored long and hard to remain on top in his sport.

LIBRA AND VIRGO

Libra (September 23–October 22) and Virgo are very different souls. Libra is extroverted and social, while Virgo is introverted and private. Libra likes to be around a lot of people, while Virgo's preferred social engagement is a small, quiet gathering of a few intimate friends. Libra loves luxury and quality and doesn't mind spending for it, while Virgo prefers functional, practical things and is basically thrifty. Virgo is decisive and Libra is indecisive. Virgo gets to work and Libra procrastinates. Libra can certainly introduce Virgo to new experiences, while Virgo can use his or her objectivity and analytical skills to help Libra make decisions. Honest communication and an acceptance of each other's differences is critical for this pairing to be successful.

AQUARIUS AND VIRGO

 Aquarius (January 20–February 18) and Virgo make an unlikely but interesting pair. Virgo is shyer and more introverted than Aquarius, but will be fascinated by Aquarius' quirkiness and diverse interests. Virgo needs security and stability, while Aquarius thrives on change and the unexpected; this carefree attitude could be a constant source of worry for Virgo. However, Virgo will be captivated by Aquarius' brilliant ideas. There will be a real meeting of the minds in this intellectual union as well as an intuitional rapport, but Aquarius will need to be aware of Virgo's shyness, and Virgo will have to give Aquarius plenty of freedom if this is to be an enduring match.

ARIES AND VIRGO

Aries (March 21–April 20) and Virgo make strange bedfellows, although the two signs are often attracted to each other. Aries is action-oriented, loves adventure

The relationship between Humphrey Bogart (Aquarius) and Lauren Bacall (Virgo) illustrates how these two signs interact. The pairing of Virgo and Aquarius seems unlikely, but Bogey and Bacall went together like salt and pepper. Bacall met Bogart when she was very young, shy, and lacking in confidence. Bogart was older and had led a rather wild life, partly because of his drinking. Bacall had a nurturing, grounding effect upon Bogart, which seemed to temper his erratic behavior, while he bolstered her confidence and introduced her to new people and experiences. Together, they lit up the silver screen. Today they are still paired in the mind of the public.

and being on the go, and is the most impulsive of the fire signs. Virgo is intellectually oriented, practical, prefers the familiar, and looks several times before leaping. Aries loves to throw caution to the winds, and is outspoken and extroverted, while Virgo is more thoughtful and introverted. These differences are exactly what pulls these two signs together; they find each other fascinating. They can also complement each other: Virgo can help Aries finish what he or she has started and act as a grounding force, while Aries can loosen Virgo up a bit and help him or her to act a little more spontaneously. There are more differences than similarities here, so compromise is the key to success.

> **SOME PROFESSIONS RULED BY VIRGO**
>
> accountant, administrator, chemist, craftsperson, dental technician, dietitian, doctor, editor, gardener, grocer, hygienist, illustrator, interpreter, librarian, masseur, mathematician, nurse, osteopath, produce dealer, scientist, secretary, statistician, stenographer, tailor, teacher

LEO AND VIRGO

A union between Leo (July 24–August 23) and Virgo could be a bit of a challenge. Leo can be self-centered, is expansive, and loves the limelight, while Virgo is modest, cautious, and prefers not to be the center of attention. Virgo's tendency to criticize could be hard on Leo's easily injured ego, so Virgo would have to hold that well-meaning tongue. Power struggles shouldn't be a problem, since Leo is king and Virgo is happy to serve, although Leo must be careful not to take advantage of hardworking Virgo. Leo's flair for the dramatic and love of the good life also may be too hard for practical, reserved Virgo to handle over the long term. Compromise and acceptance are critical here.

SAGITTARIUS AND VIRGO

 Sagittarius (November 22–December 21) and Virgo are quite different breeds. Virgo is private, carefully selects friends, and is a bit of a homebody. Sagittarius is very outgoing, has never met a stranger, and is always making social plans. Virgo is practical; Sagittarius is a dreamer. Virgo focuses on the here and now, while Sagittarius is expansive and future-oriented. However, Virgo's focus on details could blend nicely with Sagittarius' tendency to look at the big picture. Sagittarius' fine mind could woo Virgo's love of intellectual brilliance. Still, Sagittarius' independent and somewhat loose approach to matters could drive somewhat insecure, precision-loving Virgo crazy. For this match to work,

> **SHOULD HAVE BEEN SAID BY A VIRGO**
>
> There's only one real sin, and that is to persuade oneself that the second-best is anything but the second-best.
> —Doris Lessing, *The Golden Notebook*

The marriage between Virgo Sophia Loren and Sagittarius Carlo Ponti is a good example of how well these two very different signs can complement each other. Loren has described herself as an ugly duckling when she was young—such harsh self-criticism is typical of Virgo. But Ponti apparently saw her potential, which perhaps could be attributed to his optimistic, confident Sagittarian nature. They worked together on a number of films, the first of which was *Girls Marked For Danger* (1952), and Ponti helped her to develop the self-assurance she needed to succeed as an actress. She, in turn, helped ground the independent Ponti, providing a solid home base for him. The rest, as they say, is history.

Sagittarius will have to curb impulsive speech and actions, and Virgo will have to take matters less seriously.

Remember, astrology's compatibility guidelines do not mean that one sign can't have a good relationship with another. They merely indicate areas where there is potential for harmony and areas that will require patience, adjustment, and acceptance.

Practice makes perfect: Virgo Branford Marsalis employed his sign's strong sense of discipline to develop his musical talent.

BIRTHDAYS OF FAMOUS VIRGOS

River Phoenix

August 23

Shelley Long • Barbara Eden
Gene Kelly • River Phoenix

August 24

Steve Guttenberg • Marlee Matlin
Jim Capaldi • Aubrey Beardsley

August 25

Sean Connery • Leonard Bernstein • Elvis Costello • Anne Archer

August 26

Branford Marsalis • Peggy Guggenheim • Albert Sabin

August 27

Mother Teresa • Man Ray • Georg W. F. Hegel

August 28

Donald O'Connor • Johann von Goethe
Ben Gazzara • Elizabeth Seton

August 29

Richard Attenborough • Michael Jackson
Charlie Parker • Rebecca De Mornay
Oliver Wendell Holmes • Ingrid Bergman • Elliott Gould

Mother Teresa

Rebecca De Mornay

August 30

Timothy Bottoms • Raymond Massey • Mary Shelley
Jean-Claude Killy

August 31

William Saroyan • Richard Gere • Maria Montessori
Edwin Moses • Van Morrison • Itzhak Perlman

Charlie Sheen

September 1

Lily Tomlin • Seiji Ozawa • Gloria Estefan
Edgar Rice Burroughs

September 2

Peter Ueberroth • Mark Harmon
Jimmy Connors • Cleveland Amory

September 3

Charlie Sheen • Irene Papas
Anne Jackson • Valerie Perrine

September 4

Anton Bruckner • Mitzi Gaynor
Alexander Liberman • Richard Wright
Craig Claiborne

Jesse James

September 5

John Cage • Darryl F. Zanuck
Jesse James • Werner Erhard
Raquel Welch • Arthur Koestler

Raquel Welch

Patsy Cline

September 6

Jane Curtin • Swoosie Kurtz • Billy Rose
Marquis de Lafayette

September 7

Michael Feinstein • Elia Kazan
Chrissie Hynde • Buddy Holly • Peter Lawford

September 8

Peter Sellers • Sid Caesar • Patsy Cline • Freddie Mercury

September 9

Michael Keaton • Leo Tolstoy • Otis Redding • Colonel Sanders
William Bligh • Cliff Robertson

September 10

Amy Irving • Charles Kuralt • Arnold Palmer
Fay Wray • José Feliciano • Yma Sumac

September 11

Brian DePalma • Hedy Lamarr • Lola Falana
O. Henry • William X. Kienzle • D. H. Lawrence

Buddy Holly

September 12

Barry White • Linda Gray • Jesse Owens
Maurice Chevalier • Maria Muldaur

Peter Sellers

September 13

Jacqueline Bisset • Roald Dahl • Mel Torme • Claudette Colbert

September 14

Mary Crosby • Margaret Sanger • Kate Millett • Zoe Caldwell

September 15

Oliver Stone • Jackie Cooper • Agatha Christie • Hank Williams

September 16

Lauren Bacall • B. B. King • John Knowles • Peter Falk • Charlie Byrd

September 17

Ken Kesey • Roddy McDowall • Anne Bancroft

September 18

Greta Garbo • Robert Blake • Frankie Avalon

Oliver Stone

September 19

William Golding • Jeremy Irons • Paul Williams •
Twiggy • Joseph Pasternak • Brook Benton

September 20

Sophia Loren • Upton Sinclair • Anne Meara

Bill Murray

September 21

Stephen King • H. G. Wells • Bill Murray
Larry Hagman • Fannie Flagg • Catherine Oxenberg

September 22

Michael Faraday • Paul Muni • John Houseman
Shari Belafonte-Harper • Joan Jett